The Month of Saint Teresa

The Third Centenary of St. Teresa

Extracts from the Writings of the Saint

by Fr. Marin de Boylesve, S.J.

Translated and annotated
by E.A. Bucchianeri

The Month of Saint Teresa

The Third Centenary of St. Teresa
Extracts from the Writings of the Saint

by Fr. Marin de Boylesve, S.J.

Translated and annotated
by E.A. Bucchianeri

Batalha Publishers
Fatima, Portugal

This new English edition has been translated and annotated by E.A. Bucchianeri © 2022 from the French edition published in 1882 by Rene Haton, Libraire, Paris.

ISBN: 978-989-53726-1-4

Table of Contents

Thoughts of St. Peter d'Alcántara:

ဆ ✧ ര

APPENDIX

Prayers by St. Teresa

About this Edition

Fr. Marin de Boylesve's meditation selections from St. Teresa of Avila's writings celebrating her tercentenary at the time has been translated from the French edition published in 1882 by Rene Haton, Libraire, Paris. British spelling has been used.

New additions to this text include the biography of Fr. de Boylesve, the chapter headings, annotations, illustrations, and the Appendix.

E.A. Bucchianeri

About the Author

Fr. Marin de Boylesve was born on November 28, 1813 at the Château de la Coltrie in the commune of Saint-Lambert de la Potherie near Angers. He came from a distinguished aristocratic family whose name can be traced back many centuries as seen in Abbé Jean-Baptiste Ladvocat's *Dictionnaire historique portatif* (1755). Fr. Marin descended directly from Eslienne Boyliaue (or Boilyeve), the great statesman and the principal adviser of St. Louis IX, King of France. Other illustrious ancestors included intrepid knights, one in particular also named Marin joined the cause of King Henry IV. After the Battle of Arques, the king called him 'his beloved knight', granted him a heredity knighthood in 1597, then was made Seigneur de la Maurouziere in 1598 thereby granting him the right to add three gold fleur-de-lis to the top of his arms and bear the signs of the Order of St. Michel in his escutcheon. He was also appointed lieutenant-general of Anjou and councillor of state as a reward for his dedication. Another Marin Boylesve appears in the family line, the third to hold the name, and was in service to King Louis XIV as manager of his hôtel. Loyal to the French King and to their Catholic faith, many members of the family were forced to emigrate during the French Revolution, but some members stayed behind in their beloved France. Fr. de Boylesve would recall a favourite family story, of how his grandmother was imprisoned in Angers by the Revolutionaries and managed a daring escape on the road during a prisoner transfer to the local castle. While she pretended to pick up a dropped package, a solider kicked her into the ditch. She took the opportunity to flee to a nearby house. However, when they threatened to imprison those harbouring escaped prisoners, she bravely marched straight in to the Revolutionary Office and gave herself up to ensure the safety of those who sheltered her. The revolutionaries did not dare risk upsetting the populace as her father was the former mayor of Angers before the Revolution and loved by the people. They decided to let her return to her father's house.

Fr. de Boylesve was the last direct descendant of his distinguished line, having followed the call to enter the Company of Jesus, or Jesuits, which also is a remarkable story of a predestined vocation. The Jesuits were persecuted due to fears they were growing in power and wealth. Pressured by the royal courts of Europe, Pope Clement XIV suppressed the Society, forcing members of the order to renounce their vows and go into exile. They were expelled from France in 1764. Fr. de Boylesve's mother, Clémentine de Livonnière, made a solemn promise on the day of her wedding that if God permitted the Jesuits to return to France and she was granted a son, she would offer him to the order and entrust him to it. As mentioned, Fr. Marin was born in 1813, a year before 1814 when Pope Pius VII restored the Society. Tragedy struck when Marin's father died, Marin was only ten months old at the time, but keeping her promise his mother dutifully sent him for his education at the age of ten to the Jesuit Fathers of Montmorillon. The moment he arrived at the school and saw a Jesuit for the first time who happened to be the Superior of the college Fr. Michel Le Blanc, he heard an inner voice say to him: "Little one, that is what you will be."

Fr. de Boylesve entered the school as a student and was destined never to leave the Jesuits. In 1831 he turned eighteen, a year after the July Revolution of 1830, which saw the rightful king to the French throne Charles X overthrown. His heir, Henry V the 'Miracle Child', was forced into exile at the age of ten, his throne usurped by the man who had been approached to be his regent, Louis-Philippe, Duke of Orléans. The events of the times burned the hearts of the faithful as the historical church of the royal family, Saint-Germain-l'Auxerrois, was profaned. Paris was sacked, and wayside devotional crosses and shrines over large areas of France were destroyed as Catholic legitimist symbols of Charles X, even those which had no royal significance or connection to the king.

Fr. Marin had just completed his schooling when he formally announced his decision to enter the Society, the historic events of the previous year and their aftermath no doubt influencing his decision. Writing to his grandmother he declared:

"The course of my studies completed I could

not remain without doing anything. God will ask us for an exact account of all the moments He gives us. Full of this thought I ardently wished to serve my country and the Church especially. At a time when both are in such great peril, as a Frenchman and as a Christian, I felt the need to throw myself into the thick of the fray. To take place in the first rows under the banners of religion whose triumph alone can bring glory and happiness back to my homeland, to serve immediately under my first head Jesus Christ, to be one of His companions, seemed to me the most glorious at the same time as most useful for my neighbour. Immense advantages, treasures of happiness and glory, the hundredfold from this life of all that I would give to the Lord, all of these promised in the gospel by Jesus Christ, strongly attracted me to be generous. What more could I do than give myself? (...)"

His family strongly opposed, especially as he was the last direct heir to the Boylesve house, but his mother let him go despite the great sacrifice, no doubt she understood God was accepting her promise to give him to the Jesuits, and not just for his education but now was asking for his whole life, a bitter dreg for her down to the last drop of the cup.

He entered the Novitiate in 1831 at Estavayer in the canton of Fribourg in Switzerland with two other students. As they arrived at their new school, they rang the doorbell at the moment the house clock struck three. The Father who received them remarked: "You are entering at the hour of the Sacred Heart." This introduction to a new school would once again give Fr. de Boylesve a sign regarding the future work he would one day accomplish, although on this occasion he did not know it at the time. He made his first vows at the Maison du Passage on October 10, 1833. He studied philosophy and then in 1835 became a supervisor at the Collège de Mélan, a position he held for one year. He remained in the same college until 1842 where he was in succession professor of grammar, humanities and rhetoric. He thoroughly enjoyed his work with the students, writing in 1837:

"I find this job a lot of fun, despite the hardships that come with it. I have forty students; I love them and I try to spare nothing to make them good Christians, educated Christians capable of one day rendering true service to religion and to the state. It is the sight of such a noble ending that sustains and animates me." In the same letter he continues, regarding his concern for his family, "(...) what the only important thing is, is everyone behaving well and does he remember the motto of the family, RELIGIO, PATRIA? For me who gave up everything, even my name which will be extinguished in my person, I remember it, and God grant that I am consumed and that I use myself in the service of one and of the other."

Although renouncing his aristocratic life he never gave up its noble spirit represented by the family motto, an ardent loyalty to the Catholic faith of his forefathers and his country. In the title pages of his texts he included the family crest of three crosses and motto: RELIGIO, PATRIE – "Faith and Country". Those who knew him and his 'military' style ways said he was just like the loyal intrepid knights of old.

At the end of 1842 he returned to France. He took theology courses at Laval for four years. Instinctively he was drawn to the writings of St. Thomas Aquinas and steered clear of new systems that deviated from the philosophical teachings of the Seraphic Doctor. In 1846 theology training completed, Fr. Boylesve was sent by his superiors to Angers, then in his third year at Notre-Dame d'Ay. In 1848 he was appointed to Brugelette, where he occupied the chair of philosophy. One student who fondly recalled Fr. de Boylesve and his time at Brugelette said his arrival was providential. His classes were easy to follow his manner clear and crisp, but this is not all that gained the respect of the students. In 1848 they were restless as revolution was in the air, Louis-Philippe I, who had overthrown Catholic King Charles X was now in his own turn overthrown. Rising above and beyond what was required of his philosophy courses, Fr. Boylesve seized the opportunity like a knight-commander of old to direct the lazy students yet bursting with energy towards something constructive: Catholic action to fashion them into vigorous young men of service for Church and country. With his apostolic action he captivated the students with his literature classes, speaking on many subjects from philosophy, history, politics both ancient and modern. He particularly drew them with his catechism lessons on the Council of Trent, his clarity and enthusiasm captivating them.

As Fr. de Boylesve loved his students he was equally admired and loved by them, earning the nickname 'The Captain' as a mark of respect. The students composed a military style tune for his birthday, the refrain remaining popular and hummed everywhere: "Courageous Captain, lead us into battle." A student recalls: "I understood all that was apostolic about his action on us. We can sum it up by saying that he made it his mission to preach to us always and everywhere the contemplation of Saint Ignatius on the Reign of Jesus Christ as it is given in the Exercises." In 1851 Fr. Boylesve was sent to Vannes where he was made prefect of studies, his nickname 'The Captain' following him. In October 1853 he left the post and resumed teaching philosophy, a position that he would keep for a long time, either in Poitiers or in Vaugirard.

Known to be quiet and reserved when on his own, it was another matter when he was teaching or publicly speaking. He was incapable of remaining silent or softening his direct manner of expression when it was a question of truth, and did not hold back when it came to defend the Faith and the Church against unbelievers, becoming as noted like his knight-ancestor of old, charging forth to give chase and defeat any bold rascal on the field of battle albeit with his tongue and writings rather than with a literal sword. His attitude is quaintly summed up by the art critique he once gave of the statue of the fountain of St. Michael in Paris, complaining with slight annoyance that the mighty archangel was made to look too carefree and benevolent when dispatching Satan: "See then, it is that he seems to spare him!" He was also a zealous worker and relished activity. He once wrote: "I challenge my superiors to give me too much work." In addition to his religious duties and teaching, he was a prolific writer, his output seeming to have no end. He wrote on a myriad of subjects and in different genres, from devotional booklets and pamphlets to history, literature, philosophy, Biblical dramas, summaries of the Church Fathers and Doctors, his own sermons, studies of the Scriptures, Our Lady, the Exercises of St. Ignatius just to name a few, there were always more plans for further works in progress, his room filled with notes and notebooks. He was always studying as well, also making it a practise to read through the entire Bible every year. One might call him a workaholic in today's terms, but it was noted he believed in a time and a place for everything and diligently managed his hours. He enjoyed recreation time, especially going for walks, and did not sacrifice rest. Despite his zest for work, he disapproved of a few young professors who sacrificed too much sleep and recreation time for their studies, endangering their health. Yet, while sparing of his time, he was ever charitable and ready to help another all for the glory of God.

In September 1870 Fr. de Boylesve was sent to the College of Le Mans, Notre-Dame de Sainte-

Croix, when the Franco-Prussian war was raging and France suffered the indignity of invasion. The humiliation felt by the country also struck the pious and patriotic Fr. de Boylesve to the core: "I searched through the memories of my life; I do not remember ever having felt greater pain than this, not even when I learned of my mother's death. This humiliation of France, the eldest daughter of the Church, thus succumbing before Prussia, the eldest daughter of Protestantism, in the face of the whole world, is something unheard of."

The Messenger, the magazine of the Apostleship of Prayer run by the Jesuits, began spreading the visions of St. Margaret Mary, declaring the only way France would be saved from her enemies was to embrace the devotion to the Sacred Heart. The message inspired Fr. de Boylesve. He became a chaplain to the Catholic Papal Zouaves forces sent to defend the French Motherland from the Protestant invaders, giving them rousing sermons: "Clotilde, inspiring faith in Clovis, saved the Franks and slaughtered the Germans at their feet ... Joan of Arc by her standard delivered France from the English! Your standard is the Sacred Heart." The Zouaves placed the Sacred Heart on their banner. Fr. de Boylesve also busily spread Sacred Heart badges of wool for the soldiers to pin on their uniforms, for they were in high demand. A gifted and inspiring preacher, his sermons encouraged them onward, even when they were driven back in defeat by the Prussians to where the soldiers remarked: "This man can lead us to the fire tomorrow; we would gladly be killed for him."

Fr. de Boylesve is fondly remembered today in Catholic circles in France for his work as the director of the Apostleship of Prayer in Le Mans through which he contributed to the spread of devotion to the Sacred Heart. On October 17, 1870 Fr de Boylesve was appointed to preach at the Visitation of Le Mans upon St. Margaret Mary for his subject, who at the time was a Blessed. He also preached upon another mystic who had died within their own times, Mother Marie de Jesus (1797-1854) from the convent des Oiseaux of Paris who had received revelations from the Sacred Heart that were favourably recognised by the Archbishop of Paris. On June 21, 1823 the Sacred Heart revealed to Sr. Marie that He desired France be consecrated to His Sacred Heart by the King, and that a chapel be built and dedicated to Him, and the feast of the national consecration be formally celebrated every year. "After my sermon," recounts Fr. Boylesve, "the Mother Superior expressed to me her astonishment at my silence with regard to an almost similar order that Our Lord had given to Blessed Margaret Mary on June 17th, 1689. I confessed that in our college, which had barely opened for a month, I had not found the letters of the Blessed One and that I was unaware of the apparition and the order she was telling me about. I promised to make good this omission." Apparently at that time, the Sacred Heart's requests to St. Margaret Mary for a shrine and the national consecration of France by the

King were not yet widely known.

True to his word, filled with his characteristic zeal for faith and country, doing what he could to extend the reign of Jesus Christ through his beloved homeland and secure its safety, the very next day he repaired his omission by publishing a pamphlet featuring the prophecies of St. Margaret Mary and Mother Marie de Jesus entitled "Triumph of France by the Sacred Heart", composing a special prayer of consecration to be said, which the Zouaves said every Friday as hope in the Sacred Heart was sorely needed. Paris was threatened with destruction by bombardments, then starvation by the invading Prussians, having commenced a siege around the city in September 1870. The siege continued until January 1871, the citizens reduced to dire circumstances. The zoo animals were slaughtered for food, the populace also living off of stray animals and rats. While the Prussian advance had ceased, humiliation still ensued when France suffered defeat at the hands of the Prussians with the establishment of the German Empire, also losing the territory of the Alsace-Lorraine to the victors. The troubles were not over. From March to May 1871 Paris fell into the clutches of the anticlerical socialist Communards, rebels revolting against the new government of the Third Republic. Blood ran in the streets, historical buildings burned, including the Tuileries Palace. The anticlerical Communards also executed the Archbishop of Paris, Georges Darboy, fulfilling the prophecy of St. Catherine Laboure. This horrific turn of events, combined with the circulation of prophecies foretelling the destruction of Paris was at hand, the faithful no doubt felt doom hung over the city. The times were desperate. After several reprintings, including a full reproduction of the text by Fr. Ramiere in the 'Messenger' newsletter issued by the Apostleship of Prayer, more than 330,000 copies of Fr. de Boylesve's pamphlets of the 'Triumph of the Sacred Heart' were circulated. It contributed to the rapid spread devotion to the Sacred Heart and bolstered the call to have the Universal Church consecrated to the Sacred Heart, also to build a national shrine on Montmartre in atonement for the atrocities committed by the Communards who began their uprising there. Construction began in 1875, the cornerstone was laid on June 16, 1875, the day Bl. Pius IX encouraged all the faithful to pray the consecration to the Sacred Heart using the special formula composed by the Sacred Congregation of Rites for the 200th anniversary of the apparition of the Sacred Heart to St. Margaret Mary. The construction of Sacre Coeur was at last completed in 1914.

As for Fr. Boylesve, in addition to his efforts to spread devotion to the Sacred Heart he worked unceasingly at many other endeavours, not only as director of the Apostolate of Prayer in Le Mans, but also with the Confraternities of Saint Joseph such as that of the Good Death, and also the Confraternity of the Agonizing Heart, the Work of Campaigns, Conferences of St. Vincent de Paul, Workers' Circles, he still appeared to dare all and sundry that they would never be able to find enough work for him to do. He amazed all that he was never at a loss for a subject to preach upon. He could easily vary his sermons to where it appeared he never preached the same way twice, and always captured his hearers' attention. One day out of curiosity a hardened sinner walked in to listen to him preach and left a converted man. When Fr. Boylesve wasn't working, he was praying. There was no question that he maintained a deep spiritual life. He was transferred to Vaugirard in 1875, returning to Le Mans two years later in 1877. Three years later his teaching came to an end at the college there with the decree of March 29, 1880 issued by the French minister for public education prohibiting the Jesuits from engaging in their educational apostolate, only the first of several anticlerical laws that would be passed in France over the next decades. Fr. Boylesve admitted he was on the verge of tears saying his last Mass for the students in the chapel before the school closed. Yet, he remained as active as ever despite this terrible blow, preaching, giving catechisms and continuing his writing, tackling the problems of their day threatening both the Church and society. He continued working despite his old age, until the end of 1891 when his activity was curtailed. He was struck with various ailments, first a tormenting dermatitis that remained with him, then inflammation of the blood that restricted his activities for many weeks, although he managed to say Mass and continue his writing, until at last he was struck with paralysis, unable to walk or speak. Clutching his rosary and his crucifix, the ever zealous 'priest-knight' of the Vendée gave up his soul to God in February 22, 1892 and was buried in the Jesuit cemetery of Sainte-Croix.[1]

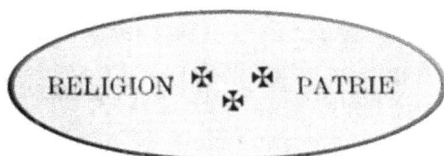

RELIGION ✠ ✠ PATRIE

---

1   Biographical information from 'Necrologie. Le Père Marin de Boylesve, in 'Lettres de Jersey', Vol. XII, No. 1 (April 1893)

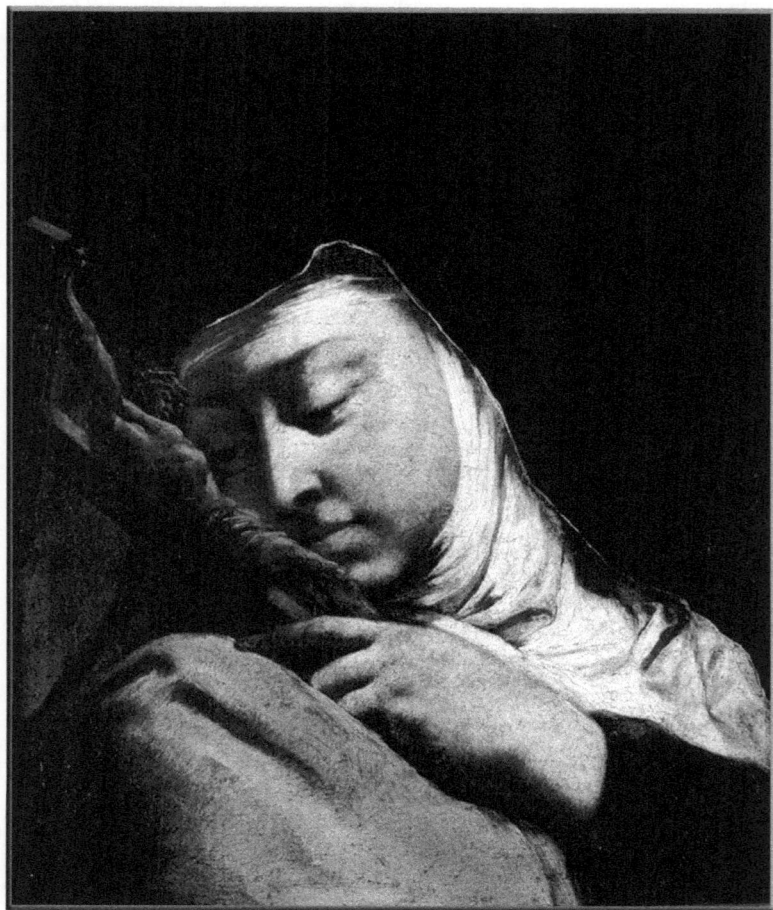

First Day

The Life of St. Teresa of Avila

Teresa was born in Avila, Spain. Her parents, no less distinguished by their piety than by their nobility, brought her up in the fear of God.

A trait of her childhood at that point foreshadowed the heroism of her future saintliness. Having read the acts of the martyrs, she was so inflamed with the fire of Divine love that she left her father's house in order to go to Africa where she hoped to give her life for the glory of Jesus Christ and for the salvation of souls.

One of her uncles brought her back; but to console herself, she devoted herself to all kinds of good works, not ceasing to testify with her tears her regret to have missed such a beautiful opportunity to die for her God. At the age of twelve she lost her mother; then she begged the most Blessed Virgin to take her place, and Mary never ceased to protect her as her daughter.

At the age of twenty she entered the nuns of Our Lady of Carmel. There, for twenty-two years, she was tried by serious illnesses and by various temptations, passing through all the exercises of Christian penance without being sustained by the sweetness of those celestial consolations which are ordinarily the portion of the saints, even in this life.

Second Day

Her Biography Continued

Adorned with truly angelic virtues, her active charity urged her to not only work for her own salvation, but also to devote herself to the salvation of her neighbour.

For this purpose, under the Divine inspiration and with the approval of Pius IV, she undertook to bring back the nuns first, then the religious of Carmel to the severity of the primitive Rule.

God in His almighty mercy visibly blessed this design. For they saw a poor girl found as many as thirty-two monasteries, not only without any human help, but also in spite of the most powerful opposition.

She never ceased to mourn the loss of the infidels and the heretics, and to appease the Divine wrath, she offered to God the holy cruelties which she exercised on her own body for their salvation.

Her heart was so ablaze with the fires of Divine love that she merited to see an angel who pierced her breast with a flaming dart, and, Jesus Himself presented His hand to her saying:

"From now on you will have for My honour the zeal of a faithful spouse."

It was also on the counsel of Our Lord that she undertook by a heroic vow to always do what appeared to her the most perfect.

She left in writing a great number of teachings of an entirely celestial wisdom which are greatly calculated to excite in souls the desire for the celestial fatherland on high.

ဆာ✧ဌ

Third Day

Conclusion of Her Biography

While she offered a continual example of all the virtues, she burned with the desire to chastise her body to the point that in spite of the illnesses with which she was constantly overwhelmed, she never stopped resorting to hair shirts, iron chains, nettles and the harshest instruments of penance. She even went so far as to roll herself in thorns. Often she said to God; "Lord, either to suffer or die," for the present life seemed to her rather a miserable death, as long as it was not given to her to drink from the source of Eternal life.

She possessed the gift of prophecy in the highest degree; and the Lord showered her so liberally with His Divine favours that often she cried out that so many blessings should be terminated, and the memory of her faults not so speedily blotted out.

Finally, consumed by the ardour of Divine love rather than by the violence of illness, and seeing herself detained in Alba on a bed of pain, she predicted the day of her death, and after having received the sacraments of the Church and exhorted her sisters to peace, to charity and to regularity, she returned her soul to God under the guise of a dove. She was sixty-seven years old. Her death occurred on October 4, 1582. Pope Gregory XIII had just removed ten days from the calendar to reform it: the next day was the 15th.

Jesus Himself, surrounded by angelic militias, had received her last breath.

At the moment of her death a dried up tree which was near her cell was covered with flowers. Her body, which has remained incorrupt to this day and surrounded by an odoriferous liquid, is the object of veneration by the faithful.

Famous for the gift of miracles before and after her death, she was included among the number of saints by Pope Gregory XV.[2]

(*Taken from the lessons of the breviary.*)

2　　　One miracle is that her heart continued to emit heat when it was taken from her body to be placed in a reliquary, showing the love her heart held for God after it was pierced with the fiery arrow by the angel. The heart was noted to burst the reliquary from the heat! In the end, the reliquary needed a lid with slits in order to let the heat escape and prevent the casing from cracking.

Fourth Day

Doing the Will of God – Detachment from Creatures

All my advice tends only to establish this principle: that we must abandon ourselves entirely to our Creator, have no other will than His, and detach ourselves from creatures.

Let your desire be to see God; your fear be of losing Him; your pain be at not possessing Him yet; your joy be of that which can lead you to Him; and you will live in great peace.

Remember you have only one soul; that you only die but once; that you only have one life which is short; that there is none but one glory that is eternal; and you will thus detach yourself from many things.

හ✧ෆ

Fifth Day

Poverty - The Practise of Holy Indifference

(Poverty) confers upon us as though it has the highest domain over the goods of this world; for it is to be master of them to (be able to) despise them.

What profit, then, do we believe we derive from pleasing creatures? And what does it matter to us that all together condemn us, provided that Thy eyes, Lord, find no fault in our soul?

Freedom of spirit: happy indifference to everything that can be said about us, whether good or bad, the soul taking no more part in it than if it were a question of a foreign person.

ഇ ✧ ര

Sixth Day

Distancing Oneself from the World – The Vanity in Seeking Worldly Honours and Position

Certainly, my adorable Master, it is no longer a sacrifice today to distance oneself from the world. Since it betrays Thee like this, what can we expect from it?

Honour is lost as soon as it is sought, principally in that which is regarded the desire for position.

St. Peter, who was just a simple fisherman, has more authority than St. Bartholomew who was the son of a king.

₲✧∛

Seventh Day

Lawful Consolations without Neglecting Duties - The Duties of Parents – All is Vanity that Does not Lead to God

So it is just, when they need consolation to procure it for them, provided that we can do it without harming the fulfilment of our duties: we can very well, by spreading the balm in their souls, maintain a perfect detachment.

What a fate awaits these fathers and mothers who, forgetting that their children belong much more to the Lord than to them, have not brought them up in His fear! When they see each other in hell, what curses will they not continue,

"Who are you?"
"I am Teresa of Jesus."
"I am Jesus of Teresa!"

and how great will be their despair for an eternity!

Let us constantly bear in mind the thought that all is vanity, and that all ends in a moment. Such a means may seem feeble, and yet it gradually imparts great vigour to the soul.

80 ✧ ca

Eighth Day

Live in a Manner so as to Not Fear Death or Illness – Love and Live for God – Reflection on the Eternity of Hell

If we do not resolve once and for all to put an end to the fear of death and the loss of health, we will never do anything.

How sweet it will be for us, at the hour of death, to see that we are going to be judged by Him Whom we will have loved above all things.

It costs so much for those who live here below in delights to pass a single night in a bad hostelry; what will that unfortunate soul will feel when it sees that it has an eternity to spend in that terrible abode (hell)?

Ninth Day

Be Generous with God – Salvation Cannot be Attained without Prayer – Charity Towards your Neighbour

(God) does not want to force our will; He receives what we give Him: but He gives Himself entirely to us only when we give ourselves entirely to Him.

We all walk towards the Fountain of Life; but there is, believe me, only one path that will lead to It, and that is prayer. Anyone who tells you otherwise is deceiving you.

When the true lovers of Jesus Christ cannot serve their neighbour by works, they fly to his aid by prayer.

₭✧℣

St. Teresa interceding for souls in Purgatory.

Tenth Day

The Effects of Prayer – Perseverance in Prayer –
Methods of Meditation – Humility Above All
if Meditation is Difficult

Prayer when compared to water; first it refreshes, it extinguishes fire, except certain fires which, on the contrary, it feeds. Thus prayer extinguishes the fire of earthly loves, it maintains and increases the fire of celestial love; second, it purifies; third, it quenches thirst.

First and above all, they (those who want to arrive at perfection, at true prayer) must have the firm and unshakeable resolution not to suspend their course until they have arrived at the Fountain of Life.

I spent more than fourteen years without even being able to meditate, except by reading. There are several people of this class: there are some who cannot meditate, even with the help of a book, but provided they remain humble I believe that in the end they will find this well reckoned to their account more than those who have many consolations in prayer.

§✧℞

Eleventh Day

*The Our Father, the Perfect Prayer - The Gospels
the Best Source for Meditation –
Often Simplicity is Best*

On the 'Our Father'. If our weakness were not so great and our devotion so cold, we would not need other ways of praying or any book treating upon prayer.

The words of the Gospel have always brought me to meditation more than the best written works, especially when there were no well-approved authors, for then I had no desire to read them.

Often too many books only serve to extinguish the fervour with which we must recite this holy prayer.[3]

ॐ ✧ ☙

---

3   Note: she later says books are useful for meditation, therefore in this case she obviously means too many *explanatory* or theological books on the prayer itself that may cause one to approach it from an intellectual 'academic' angle and in the end cause a negative outcome. Prayer springs from the heart, not just the mind, hence, this may explain her observation why too many books can extinguish heartfelt fervour.

Twelfth Day

Advice on How to Pray – Interior Recollection

Eyes closed during prayer, an excellent and admirably useful custom.

Often recalling one's senses within oneself, gradually making oneself master of oneself, remembering that they have in the depths of their heart Someone to speak to; one can, if one wishes, never separate themselves from this Divine company. Let the soul practice this several times a day, I assure you that with the assistance of Our Lord you will come to the end in a year, and perhaps in six months.[4]

(Mental prayer) consists only of collecting ourselves within ourselves, in order to understand well what we are saying, how great is He to Whom we have the boldness to speak.

ℰℴ ✧ ℭℛ

---

4   I.e. she appears to be saying that if one practices this interior recollection regularly, with the Lord's help, within six months to a year they will become a master over their interior prayer life.

Thirteenth Day

Advice on How to Pray Continued – Holy Images as a Spiritual Help – Spiritual Books

It is in our power to accustom ourselves to walking in the presence of Our Lord: let us make generous efforts, and we shall in the end have the consolation of enjoying the company of this True Master of our souls.

One way that will help you to stand in the presence of Our Lord is to have an image of this adorable Master that suits your taste: usually have it before your eyes.

Here is another very useful means of conversing with Our Lord, and that is to take a book written in the vernacular. By reading it your mind will recollect more easily.[5]

ഇ✧ര

---

5   I.e. this advice was given at a time when clergy and religious were taught Latin and read Latin texts. The saint is suggesting for the sake of focused prayer and meditation that a vernacular book be used rather than a Latin one so the idea meditated upon is clearer to the mind – more often than not a learned language is not comprehended as fluently as a speaker's first language.

Fourteenth Day

Offering Your Daily Works to God – Working Towards Spiritual Perfection: Form the Habit of Continually Examining Your Conscience

Do all things as if you really saw Our Lord present before you; the soul thus acquires great treasures of merit.

Direct all your actions towards God, make an offering to Him, and ask Him that it be for His honour and for His glory.

At every hour and with every action you take, examine your conscience; and after having seen your faults, blemishes, with the help of God, correct yourself of them; by this way you will arrive at perfection.

ഔ✧ଷ

Fifteenth Day

The Importance of Prayer After Communion – Union with Christ at Communion – True Freedom Equals Spiritual Detachment – The Supernatural Prayer of Quietude

Do not waste the hour following Holy Communion; it is an excellent time to negotiate and to manage the interests of your soul.[6]

Since Jesus Christ Himself is within you, as soon as you have received the Holy Eucharist close your bodily eyes to open those of your soul, and then look at Him; He is in the middle of your heart.

Anything that binds us in such a way as to deprive us of the use of reason must be suspect to us: never thereby will we arrive at freedom of the mind; for one of the characteristics of this freedom is to find God in all things and to rise to Him by means of creatures.[7]

---

6   I.e. this is the most efficacious time to bring your requests and needs to the Lord.

7   I.e. the saint says regarding the interior life we must be suspicious of anything that binds us in a way that impairs our proper use of reason, we can only arrive at true freedom of mind with the proper use of reason. She then points out an example of the proper use: that we are to see God in all things, and they are meant to

This prayer (of quietude) is supernatural, and consequently above all our industries and all our efforts.[8]

ഇൗ ✧ ൠ

Sixteenth-Day

Advice – How to Reap Spiritual Fruit from Meditation – Practising Inner Discretion – The Soul Advances by Love, How to Acquire this Love

Have present during the day what you meditated on in the morning; be faithful to this

---

help us rise to Him, we are not meant to be bound by them. Basically, we are to avoid anything that causes us to form base or worldly attachments that prevent the soul from ascending to God.

8   Quietude in St. Teresa's writings mean a supernatural state of prayer that is *partially* passive where the will is seized by God, *while the other faculties are still active* but calmed. Action is still present in the soul. The soul realizes that it is near to God and enjoys complete peace, while the intellect enjoys a gentle repose and experiences a keen satisfaction in God's presence.   This is not to be confused with the condemned heresy of 'quietism', that proposes a 'self annihilation' with the 'total absorption' of the soul into the Divine Essence, with the mind wholly inactive and unable to think on its own account.

practice, you will reap great fruit.

Do not show your inner devotion, unless there is great necessity: 'My secret is mine,' said St. Francis and St. Bernard.

The advancement of the soul does not consist in thinking much, but in loving much. How, however, to acquire this love? By making a firm determination to work and suffer, and indeed doing so when the occasion presents itself.

ော✧ၼ

Seventeenth Day

The Lord Notices the Least Action Done for Him – Christ is a Just Leader and Appoints Tasks Accordingly - How He Distributes His Crosses – The Life of a Good Religious

He (Our Lord) notices with sovereign exactitude our least services: if we only raise our eyes to heaven with a remembrance of the heart for Him, do not fear that He will leave this action without reward.

(Jesus Christ). He is an incomparable

captain who, being Himself a witness to the generous deeds of His soldiers, knows the merit of each of them and gives them offices and employments as He deems them worthy.

(Regarding crosses). To those He loves more, He gives more; and to those He loves less, He gives less.

The life of a good religious ... it is a long martyrdom.

ഇ✧ൽ

Eighteenth Day

The Humility of Christ – The Nature of True Humility – Recognising False Humility - Strong Souls – Generous Souls

Wherein hast Thou placed Thy honour, O Master worthy of the eternal respect of heaven and earth? Hast Thou lost it by humbling Thyself unto death? No, Lord; it is by this, on the contrary, that Thou hast exalted us all.

True humility, far from throwing the soul into trouble and anguish, expands it in holiness

St. Teresa and St. John of the Cross

and makes it more capable of working in the service of God.

The (false) humility of which the devil is the author disturbs and agitates.

He (the demon) fears nothing so much as strong and resolute souls.

Generous souls always feel much more inclined to give than to receive, and they feel this imperative necessity with regard to the Creator Himself. It is to this way of loving that the name of love legitimately belongs.

$\infty \diamondsuit \infty$

Nineteenth Day

True Love of Neighbour – The Salvation of Souls

When holy souls love a person, they work with a holy passion to bring them to love God... (because) they know that if the Divine charity is not in them, death must forever break the bond that unites them.

We constantly tremble that this dear soul will be lost, and that we will be forced to part with them forever.

I feel my heart breaking at the sight of so many souls being lost...I wish at least that I do not see any more become lost. O my daughters in Jesus Christ, join me in asking...for this grace from the Divine Master. This is your vocation; that is your business; these must be all your desires ... it is this that you must not stop asking God.

ℰ✧ℭ

Twentieth Day

The Delight of Winning Souls for the Greater Glory of God – The Salvation of Souls is the Most Important Apostolic Mission for a Carmelite (and all Christians)

When I read the lives of the saints, the story of the apostolic labours of those who won worshippers for God and populated Heaven excites my devotion, my tears, my envy,[9] far more than the tableau of all the torments endured by the martyrs.

---

9   No doubt she means a holy 'envy' in that the apostles won so many souls for God, which fills her with a holy zeal for the salvation of souls and attracts her far more than the stories of the torments endured by the martyrs.

And what does it matter to me to remain until the Day of Judgement in purgatory, if by my prayers I save a single soul; if especially by working for the spiritual advancement of many, I bring greater glory to my God.

I have just indicated to you the goal to which you must relate your prayers, your desires, your disciplines, your fasts: from the day that you cease to relate them to this our apostolic goal, know that you are not doing what Jesus Christ expects of you, and that you are not fulfilling the purpose for which he has brought you together in Carmel.

80 ✧ 03

Twenty-First Day

Aiming for Perfection – Praying for the Defenders of the Church

You have just seen the greatness of the business in which we claim to succeed. What will help us mightily is to hold our thoughts high; we will thus endeavour to maintain our works at the same level. Let us observe our rule with perfect care.

It seemed to me that by occupying ourselves

entirely in praying for the defenders of the Church, for the preachers and scholars who fight for her, we would come according to our power to the aid of this adorable Master so unworthily persecuted.

Do not imagine that it is useless to be thus continually occupied in praying to God, for the defenders of His Church... Believe me, no prayer is better or more profitable.

ও✧ଓ

Twenty-Second Day

The Importance of Praying that Church Leaders are Given Courage and Virtue – Perseverance in Virtue Strengthens those who Defend the Church

I would be ready to write the same things a hundred times if I believed them to be of any use for the good of souls.

I come back to the main point, that is to say to the end that Our Lord proposed by bringing us together in this house. This end, as I said, is the salvation of souls. So what we have to ask God....is that He give to the captains of this place (of the Church which she compared to a fortress), that is to say to the preachers and to the theologians, a manly courage and an eminent virtue.

It is by a great constancy in the study and in the practice of virtue, that they have made themselves capable of defending the cause of the Church.

℘✧ℭ

Twenty-Third Day

Knowledge Gives Light – The Importance of Attaining Virtue for Spiritual Advancement

Knowledge is of admirable help to give light in all things.

Virtue has in itself such a powerful charm! It is enough to put it before the eyes so that it wins the affection.

Do you think it takes little virtue to condescend outwardly to the customs of the world and to be at the same time, in one's heart, not only distant from the world, but also an enemy of the world?

Twenty-Fourth Day

Why God Seems Slow to Act Great Wonders in Our Favour – Courage is Needed – The Importance of Knowing God

Lord, it is not due to Thee that those who love Thee do not do great things. The obstacle is our cowardice, our pusillanimity; we do not know how to undertake anything for Thy glory, without mingling with it a thousand fears, a thousand human considerations. That is why, O my God, Thou display neither the power of Thy arm, nor the greatness of seeing wonders: for who has more pleasure than Thee in giving, when Thou finds one on whom to pour out Thy largesse, and Who rewards services with more munificence?

My God, that all the obstacles here below are a small thing, when it pleases Thee to grant us courage.

The more one knows God, the fewer difficulties one finds in what one undertakes for His service.

ഇ✧Ꭷ

The first miracle of St. Teresa, the resurrection of her nephew Don Gonzalo Ovalle, who was crushed beneath a wall that fell. After praying a few minutes while holding him, he came back to life.

Twenty-Fifth Day

*God Raises Up Men of Truth in Times of Error —
One Such Man Preaching Truth Prevails Over the
Thousands in Error — The Demon's Method of
Discrediting the Spiritually Perfect*

In these times of trouble and mass dispute where the demon leads, it seems, all men are dazzled by the (false) appearance of a good zeal, what does God need? To open the eyes of so many blind people, He raises up a man. O power of my God! He alone, this man teaching the truth, prevails over legions of others who do not know it.

The world is astonished at the slightest faults of (those who are) perfect, and is not astonished to see a hundred thousand of these slaves of the age manifestly immersed in public sins. In a sense, the world reasons correctly: the faults of the good are something rare and which should astonish.

Nothing is more ordinary to humans than to pass without thinking over what they see every day, and marvel at what they seldom or hardly ever see. The demon inspires this astonishment: he has a great interest in this, because a single soul which arrives at perfection takes away a great number of others.

Twenty-Sixth Day

On Those Who Truly Love God – The Danger of
Useless Fear in the Interior Life - Crippling
Scruples – Scrupulous Souls Become Useless
to Themselves and Others

Those who truly love God, love all that is good, want all that is good, praise all that is good, always unite with the good, support them, defend them.

Avoid fear and interior embarrassment: the soul that abandons itself to it experiences very great difficulties for every kind of good; often they fall into scruples, and thus become useless for themselves and for others.

The sight of this embarrassment and this constraint frightens us and makes us drop our arms. We will gladly grant that this soul walks in a better way, but we will lose all desire to follow it.

---

10   I.e. St. Teresa seems to be saying here if it is believed a certain soul is on the good path towards the interior life, but if it is also noticed they are suffering inner fear, embarrassments, or crippling scruples hindering their forward progress, nobody will desire to follow their example as fear does not inspire imitation, everybody loses the courage to follow that soul's example despite the good path they are on. Hence, souls caught in this type of crippling fear become useless with

Try to conduct yourself in such a way that people feel drawn to share your way of living and acting.

ဆာ✧ရ

Twenty-Seventh Day

Love of Neighbour – Take the Beam Out of Your Own Eye – Be Not Dainty or Complain Over Food – Practise Holy Restraint in Speaking

Never listen to ill spoken of anyone and never say anything, except about yourself.[11]

Do not think of the faults of others, but think of their virtues and of your own faults.

Whether food is well or badly prepared, do not complain, remembering the gall and the vinegar that were presented to Jesus Christ.

When you are with several people, always speak little.[12]

---

regards to helping others as well as themselves.

11   I.e., do not listen to or engage in gossip about your neighbour and their faults. Rather, confess and speak of your own faults and failings first.   Take the beam out of your eye first, etc.

12   I.e. advice on learning not to engage in gossip and to avoid idle words, each idle word must be accounted for in our judgement.   The wise speak little. "A peaceable

Twenty-Eighth Day

Bearing Wrongs Patiently – Avoiding Idle Curiosity – Refrain from Giving Your Opinion Unless Needed - Practise Holy Solitude

Never give excuses unless there is a strong reason to do so.[13]

Avoid speaking, or informing yourself with curiosity, of things that do not concern you.

Never get involved in giving your opinion on anything, unless you are asked to or charity requires it.

Keep faithfully to your cell and do not leave it without reason; and when you are forced to leave, ask God for the grace not to offend Him.[14]

---

tongue is a tree of life, but that which is immoderate shall crush the spirit." (Proverbs 15:4) Also, this is advice on the virtue of humility, to practise not being the centre of attention.

13   I.e. do not try to defend or excuse yourself, (against accusations? I.e. petty accusation or remarks, etc), it is a spiritual act of mercy to bear wrongs patiently. However, as St Teresa shows, there are times when you need to speak in your own defense, if the accusation is indeed grave and / or requires you to do so to preserve your good name and reputation for example.

14   While this was advice was given by St. Teresa for religious in a Carmelite monastery, Fr. de Boylesve often shows in his works that the laity too can live to a certain

Twenty-Ninth Day

Devotion to St. Joseph

Although you honour several saints as your advocates in heaven, nevertheless have a special devotion to St. Joseph, because he is very powerful with God.

I took for an advocate and protector the glorious St. Joseph. He always answered me beyond my prayers and my hopes. I do not remember ever asking him for anything until now that he did not grant it to me.

I do not know one of his servants who does not make new progress in virtue every day. If anyone doubts his power or his concern for those who honour him, I beg them to try it: soon they will be convinced.

ℰ✧ℭ

---

degree in holy solitude in order to practice detachment from the world. He quotes the example of the holy solitude of the Blessed Virgin in Nazareth, how she stayed humbly hidden in her daily duties and was not seen in public unless necessity or charity demanded it, such as the Visitation, and even then when she left the sanctuary of her home, she did not get distracted on the way, she went and returned to the solitude of her home with no distraction or deviation from her course.

The Virgin placing St. Teresa under St. Joseph's protection.

Thirtieth Day

General Idea about St. Teresa

Bourdaloue sees in St. Teresa:

1, The body sacrificed by mortification;
2, The soul transformed by prayer;

1: Mortification. Luther undertakes a reform which is the abolition of penance for all Christians and (abolition) of celibacy for priests and religious.

(In contrast), St. Teresa undertakes a reformation which is the most complete immolation of the flesh: *aut pati, aut mori.*

2: Prayer. It is a gift from God; but first one can and one must be disposed towards it and earn it by stubborn fidelity: seek and you will find. St. Teresa searched and waited for twenty-two years. Second, one must receive it according to the example of St. Teresa with humility and with docility from the director who represents God.[15] 3rd, One must discern the true and false spirit of prayer. The marks of true spirit are: faith and obedience to the Church, zeal for the Church, charity towards one's neighbour, regularity.

---

15 I.e. humble obedience to the spiritual director God grants you.

MISERICORDIAS DOMINI· INÆTERNVM CANTABO·

Thirty-First Day

Prayer to St. Teresa According to the Hymns of Her Feast Day

Regis superni

God's messenger, Teresa,
Thou leav'st thy father's home
To bring mankind to Jesus
Or gain sweet martyrdom.

But milder death awaits thee,
And fonder pains are thine,
God's blessed Angel wounds thee
With fire of love divine.

Sweet virgin, love's pure victim,
So fire our souls with love,
And lead thy trusting people
Safe to the realms above.

Give glory to the Father,
The Spirit and the Son,
One Trinity, one Godhead,
While endless ages run.

Haec est dies

(From the Breviary)

This is the day, when, filled with love,
And shining like a heavn'ly dove,
The spirit of Teresa flies
To temples high above the skies.

And then she hears the bridegroom's voice:
"The wedding of the Lamb, rejoice!
Come, sister, from Mount Carmel's height.
Come to your crown of glory bright."

May all the virgins blest adore
O Bridegroom Jesus, evermore,
And sing You wedding songs of praise
Throughout the everlasting days.

Prayer:

Hear us, O God our Saviour, and grant that we, rejoicing on this feast of your blessed virgin St. Teresa, be nourished with the food of heavenly doctrine and imbued with the feelings of tender devotion.   Through Jesus Christ Our Saviour. Amen.

ം ✧ രു

Thoughts of St. Peter d'Alcántara:[16]
On Prayer

We take advantage of the space that remains to complete the admirable counsels of the Seraphic St. Teresa with some advice from another Seraphic individual who was one of the most skilful directors of the saint.

✧

The Soul of Jesus Christ offers contemplation a much wider field than His sacred Body, either in relation to the feeling of suffering, or in relation to the other feelings which filled It and the thoughts which occupied It. (*Treatise on prayer,* Ch IV.)

In order to make His apostles understand that the sufferings of His soul were not less than those which were beginning to appear externally, He said to them these words imprinted with such deep pain: 'My soul is sorrowful unto death.'. (*Meditation on the prayer in the garden.*)

---

16   St. Peter d'Alcántara (1499-1562) was a Spanish Franciscan friar who encouraged St. Teresa in her reform of the Carmelite Order, advising her to found her first monastery at Avila. He had the gift of levitation, miracles and prophecy. He died on his knees while praying. He was canonized in 1669.

If the flesh, which endured only by repercussion these pains, which was the (sweat of blood), what must have happened in the soul which endured them directly?

The blow: consider those eyes so serene, that brow so calm, that soul most holy, so humble.

To imagine these things happen inside our heart. Since cities and kingdoms are comfortable in the heart, it will be much easier for it to contain the representation of these mysteries. This method will greatly help the soul to occupy herself within herself. Like the bee which, shut up in its hive, makes its honeycomb. (Ch. VIII.)[17]

After the work of meditation and of prayer let oneself rest in contemplation. Let him reject all imaginations that present themselves to him, let him appease reason, let him calm memory and fix it on Our Lord, considering that he is in His presence. Let him then leave aside all particular consideration of the things of God and be content with the knowledge that faith gives; that he applies the will and love; it is love alone which ignites and in itself is the fruit of all meditation. For what the understanding can know of God is almost nothing, while the will can love much.

---

17   I.e. advice to practice imagining the Gospel scenes in the deep, private interior of the heart.

Man will therefore shut himself up within himself in the centre of his soul, where the image of God is, and there he will listen to this great God as if he were listening to someone who would speak to him from the height of a tower, or as if he possessed Him in the middle of his heart, or as if, in this whole universe, there was only his soul, alone with God alone.

He should even lose the memory of himself and of what he is doing, because, as a poet said:
The perfect prayer is that in which the one who prays does not remember that he is in prayer.

Just as, says St. Augustine, one must abandon vocal prayer (unless they be prayers of obligation), when it is an obstacle to devotion, so one must abandon meditation when it is an obstacle to contemplation. (8th avis.)

The contemplative must be deaf, blind and dumb, because the less he spreads himself outside, the more he will be collected within himself. (*Treatise on Devotion*, Ch. II).

To walk in the presence of God, multiply those prayers that St. Augustine called jaculatory prayers, is a means to advance much in a short time. (Ibid.)

Resolution. – The greatest glory is to imitate Jesus in His virtues. Now one of His most eminent virtues is to have endured all that He suffered, without admitting into His soul any kind of consolation. (Ibid., Ch. IV., 1st opinion.)

When sleep comes from some infirmity, we need not grieve about it since it is not our fault. Let us not give in entirely, but let us do what is in our power, so as not to lose entirely prayer without which there is in this life neither assurance nor joy. (Ibid. ch. IV. 6th avis.)

The end of all exercises and of all spiritual life is obedience to the commandments of God, the the accomplishment of the Divine Will. (Ibid. Ch. V., 1st avis.)

I want no other proof of this than the divine prayer contained in the psalm *'Beati immaculati in via.'* This psalm, composed of seventy-six verses, and the longest of the psalter, contains not a verse which does not speak of the law of God, and the exact observance of His commandments. (Ibid. Ch. V. 1st avis.)[18]

The true proof of advancement is not the taste for prayer, but patience in tribulation, self-denial, and the fulfilment of the Divine Law. (ibid.).

---

18   Psalm 118 according to the Douay-Rheims Bible, which has 176 verses. Obviously, the Bible used by St. Peter d'Alcantra had a different numbering. See the Appendix for the Psalm.

APPENDIX

Prayers by St. Teresa

"Let Nothing Disturb You" - Prayer for Inner Peace by St. Teresa

(Also Known as 'St. Teresa's Bookmark', as she kept it in her breviary.)

Let nothing disturb you,
Let nothing frighten you,
All things are passing away:
God never changes.
Patience obtains all things
Whoever has God lacks nothing;
God alone suffices. Amen.

৶ ✧ ৎ

When crosses would afflict thee,
Oh! let thy watchword be,
Thy holy Mother's lesson,
"Let nothing trouble thee."

If darkness round thee gathers,
And fills thy soul with fear,

"Let nothing e'er affright thee,"
She whispers in thy ear.

In every joy or sorrow
Which meets thee day by day,
She bids thee to remember
That all things pass away."

If lonely or forsaken,
By friends thou art forgot,
Thy Spouse, she doth remind thee,
"Is one that changeth not."

When hope within thee wavers,
And distant seems the goal,
How patience winneth all things,
She tells thy weary soul,

That nothing in the wide world
Is needful unto one
Whose happy soul possesses
God's own eternal Son.

To drink the living waters
At any cost or price,
To quench thy thirst she whispers,
"God only doth suffice."

Oh! sweet, seraphic Mother,
May these dear words of thine
Help to unite me closer
Unto my Spouse divine!

Prayer to Redeem Lost Time

O my God! Source of all mercy! I acknowledge Thy sovereign power. While recalling the wasted years that are past, I believe that Thou, Lord, can in an instant turn this loss to gain. Miserable as I am, yet I firmly believe that Thou can do all things. Please restore to me the time lost, giving me Thy grace, both now and in the future, that I may appear before Thee in wedding garments. Amen.

ഇ✧ൟ

Prayer to Accomplish God's Will

Lord, grant that I may always allow myself to be guided by Thee, always follow Thy plans, and perfectly accomplish Thy Holy Will. Grant that in all things, great and small, today and all the days of my life, I may do whatever Thou dost require of me.

Help me respond to the slightest prompting of Thy grace, so that I may be Thy trustworthy instrument for Thy honour. May Thy Will be done in time and in eternity by me, in me, and through me. Amen.

ဆ✧ದ

Prayer to Endure Suffering

Teach me, my God, to suffer in peace the afflictions which Thou send me that my soul may emerge from the crucible like gold, both brighter and purer, to find Thee within me. Trials like these, which at present seem unbearable, will eventually become light, and I shall be anxious to suffer again, if by so doing I can render Thee greater service. And however numerous may be my troubles and persecutions ... they will all work together for my greater gain though I do not myself bear them as they should be borne, but in a way which is most imperfect.   Amen.

ဆ✧ದ

စာ✧ၹ

<u>Whatever God Wills</u>

Majestic Sovereign, timeless Wisdom,
Thy kindness melts my hard, cold soul.
Handsome lover, selfless giver,
Thy beauty fills my dull, sad eyes.
I am Thine, Thou didst make me.
I am Thine, Thou didst call me.
I am Thine, Thou didst save me.
I am Thine, Thou dost love me.
I will never leave Thy presence.
Give me death, give me life.
Give me sickness, give me health.
Give me honour, give me shame.
Give me weakness, give me strength.
I will have whatever Thou givest. Amen

စာ✧ၹ

A Prayer to Age Gracefully

Lord, Thou knowest better than I myself that I am growing older and will someday be old. Keep me from the fatal habit of thinking I must say something on every subject and on every occasion. Release me from craving to straighten out the affairs of others. Make me thoughtful but not moody; helpful but not demanding. With my vast store of wisdom, it seems a pity not to use it all; but Thou knowest, Lord, that I want but a few friends at the end. Keep my mind free from the recital of endless details; give me wings to get to the point. Seal my lips on my aches and pains; they are increasing, and love of rehearsing them is becoming sweeter as the years go by. I dare not ask for improved memory, but for a growing humility and a lessening of stubborn self-sureness when my memory seems to clash with the memories of others. Teach me the glorious lesson that occasionally I may be mistaken. Keep me reasonably sweet, for a sour old person is one of the crowning works of the devil. Give me the ability to see good things in unexpected places and talents in unexpected people; and give, O Lord, the grace to tell them so.   Amen.

ℰ✧ℛ

Litany to St. Teresa

Lord, *have mercy on us.*
Christ, *have mercy on us.*
Lord, *have mercy on us.*
Christ, *hear us.*
Christ, *graciously hear us.*
God, the Father of heaven,
Have mercy on us.
God the Son, Redeemer of the world,
Have mercy on us.
God the Holy Ghost, the Sanctifier,
Have mercy on us.
Holy Trinity, one God,
Have mercy on us.

Holy Mary, Mother of God, ***Pray for us, etc.***
*

Holy Mary, Our Lady of Mount Carmel, *
Saint Teresa of Avila, *
St. Teresa, whose heart was
        transverberated by the love of God, *
St. Teresa, most humble servant of God, *
St. Teresa, most zealous for the glory of God, *
St. Teresa, woman truly strong in mind, *
St. Teresa, truly detached from
        all created objects, *

St. Teresa, great light of the Catholic Church, *
St. Teresa, reformer and glory
      of the Carmelite Order, *
St. Teresa, Queen of Mystical Theology, *
St. Teresa, lustrous name of Avila and Spain, *
St. Teresa, who didst forever glorify
      the name of Teresa, *
St. Teresa, wishing to suffer or to die, *
St. Teresa, exclaiming, O Lord, how sweet and
      pleasing are Thy ways! *
St. Teresa, desiring so much the
      salvation of souls, *
St. Teresa, tasting and seeing how sweet is the
      Lord, even in this vale of miseries, *
St. Teresa, exclaiming, O death, who can fear
thee who art the way to true life! *
St. Teresa, true lover of the Cross of Christ, *
St. Teresa, who didst live to love, died to love,
      and wilt love eternally, *

      Lamb of God, Who takest away the sins
of the world:
      Spare us, O Lord.
Lamb of God, Who takest away the sins of the
world:
      Hear us, O Lord.
      Lamb of God, Who takest away the sins
of the world:
      Have mercy on us.

V. Pray for us, O holy Saint Teresa:
R. That we may be made worthy of the promises of Christ.

Let us pray

O God, Who didst replenish the heart of Thy blessed servant St. Teresa with the treasures of Thy divine love: grant that, like her, we may love Thee and suffer all things for Thee and in union with Thee; that we may gain souls to Thee, and secure our own; and this we beg through the merits of our Saviour and the intercession of Thy glorious virgin Teresa. Amen.

80✧ଔ

Indulgenced Prayer to St. Teresa by St. Alphonsus de Liguori

*(An indulgence of 300 days.
A plenary indulgence on the usual conditions,
if this prayer is said devoutly
every day for a month.)*

O Saint Teresa, seraphic Virgin, beloved spouse of thy crucified Lord, thou who on earth didst burn with a love so intense toward thy God and my God, and now dost glow with a brighter and purer flame in paradise: obtain for me also, I beseech thee, a spark of that same holy fire which shall cause me to forget the world, all things created, and even myself; for thou didst ever avidly desire to see Him loved by all men. Grant that my every thought and desire and affection may be continually directed to doing the will of God, the supreme Good, whether I am in joy or in pain, for He is worthy to be loved and obeyed forever. Obtain for me this grace, thou who art so powerful with God; may I be all on fire, like thee, with the holy love of God. Amen.

৩ ✧ ৫

Novena to St. Teresa
by St. Alphonsus Liguori

Day 1 - O most amiable Lord Jesus Christ! We thank Thee for the great gift of faith and devotion to the Most Blessed Sacrament which Thou gave to Thy servant Teresa. We pray that by Thy merits and those of Thy faithful spouse, that we may receive the gift of faith and of a fervent devotion toward the most Blessed Sacrament, through which Thou give Thyself to us.

Our Father... Hail Mary... Glory be...

St. Teresa, pray for us.

That we may become worthy of the promises of Christ.

Let us pray:

Graciously hear us, O God of our salvation, that as we rejoice in the commemoration of the blessed virgin Teresa, so we may be nourished by her heavenly doctrine, and obtain the fervour of tender devotion; through our Lord Jesus Christ, Thy Son, Who lives and reigns with Thee in the unity of the Holy Spirit, one God forever and ever. Amen.

Day 2 - O most merciful Lord Jesus Christ! We thank Thee for the great gift of hope which Thou granted to Thy beloved Teresa. Grant, we pray, that by Thy merits and those of Thy holy spouse, that we may receive confidence in Thy goodness by reason of Thy Precious Blood, which Thou shed for our salvation.

Our Father... Hail Mary... Glory be...

St. Teresa, pray for us.

That we may become worthy of the promises of Christ.

Let us pray:

Graciously hear us, O God of our salvation, that as we rejoice in the commemoration of the blessed virgin Teresa, so we may be nourished by her heavenly doctrine, and obtain the fervour of tender devotion; through our Lord Jesus Christ, Thy Son, Who lives and reigns with Thee in the unity of the Holy Spirit, one God forever and ever. Amen.

Day 3 - O most loving Lord Jesus Christ! We thank Thee for the great gift of love which Thou bestowed on Thy bride Teresa. We pray that by Thy merits, and by those of Thy most loving spouse, that we may receive the crowning gift of Thy perfect love.

Our Father...Hail Mary...Glory be...

St. Teresa, pray for us.

That we may become worthy of the promises of Christ.

Let us pray:

Graciously hear us, O God of our salvation, that as we rejoice in the commemoration of the blessed virgin Teresa, so we may be nourished by her heavenly doctrine, and obtain the fervour of tender devotion; through our Lord Jesus Christ, Thy Son, Who lives and reigns with Thee in the unity of the Holy Spirit, one God forever and ever. Amen.

Day 4 - O most sweet Lord Jesus Christ! We thank Thee for the gift of determination and resolution which Thou gave to Thy beloved Teresa. Grant, we pray, that by Thy merits and those of Thy most generous spouse, that we may receive the determination and resolution to please Thee above all things.

Our Father...Hail Mary...Glory be...

St. Teresa, pray for us.

That we may become worthy of the promises of Christ.

Let us pray:

Graciously hear us, O God of our salvation, that as we rejoice in the commemoration of the blessed virgin Teresa, so we may be nourished by her heavenly doctrine, and obtain the fervour of tender devotion; through our Lord Jesus Christ, Thy Son, Who lives and reigns with Thee in the unity of the Holy Spirit, one God forever and ever. Amen.

Day 5 - O most kind Lord Jesus Christ! We thank Thee for the great gift of humility which Thou gave to Your beloved Teresa. Grant, we pray, that by Thy merits and by those of Thy most humble spouse, that we may receive the grace of true humility, which may make us rejoice in humiliation and prefer contempt before every honour.

Our Father...Hail Mary...Glory be...

St. Teresa, pray for us.

That we may become worthy of the promises of Christ.

Let us pray:

Graciously hear us, O God of our salvation, that as we rejoice in the commemoration of the blessed virgin Teresa, so we may be nourished by her heavenly doctrine, and obtain the fervour of tender devotion; through our Lord Jesus Christ, Thy Son, Who lives and reigns with Thee in the unity of the Holy Spirit, one God forever and ever. Amen.

Day 6 - O most bountiful Lord Jesus Christ! We thank You for the gift of devotion to Thy mother Mary and her holy spouse Joseph, which Thou gave to Thy beloved Teresa. Grant, we pray, that by Thy merits and by those of Thy beloved spouse, that we may receive the grace of this same devotion.

Our Father...Hail Mary...Glory be...

St. Teresa, pray for us.

That we may become worthy of the promises of Christ.

Let us pray:

Graciously hear us, O God of our salvation, that as we rejoice in the commemoration of the blessed virgin Teresa, so we may be nourished by her heavenly doctrine, and obtain the fervour of tender devotion; through our Lord Jesus Christ, Thy Son, Who lives and reigns with Thee in the unity of the Holy Spirit, one God forever and ever. Amen.

Day 7 - O most loving Lord Jesus Christ! We thank Thee for the gift of the wounded heart of Thy beloved Teresa. We pray that by Thy merits, and by those of Thy seraphic spouse, that we may receive the same wound of love, so that we may love Thee and give Thee our whole mind and love.

Our Father...Hail Mary...Glory be...

St. Teresa, pray for us.

That we may become worthy of the promises of Christ.

Let us pray:

Graciously hear us, O God of our salvation, that as we rejoice in the commemoration of the blessed virgin Teresa, so we may be nourished by her heavenly doctrine, and obtain the fervour of tender devotion; through our Lord Jesus Christ, Thy Son, Who lives and reigns with Thee in the unity of the Holy Spirit, one God forever and ever. Amen.

Day 8 - O most beloved Lord Jesus Christ! Thou bestowed a holy death upon Thy beloved servant Teresa. We pray that by Thy merits, and those of Thy most constant spouse, to grant us the grace of a holy death, that we may possess Thee eternally in Heaven.

Our Father... Hail Mary...Glory be...

St. Teresa, pray for us.

That we may become worthy of the promises of Christ.

Let us pray:

Graciously hear us, O God of our salvation, that as we rejoice in the commemoration of the blessed virgin Teresa, so we may be nourished by her heavenly doctrine, and obtain the fervour of tender devotion; through our Lord Jesus Christ, Thy Son, Who lives and reigns with Thee in the unity of the Holy Spirit, one God forever and ever. Amen.

Day 9 - Lord Jesus Christ, we thank Thee for the gift of the holy death of Thy beloved spouse Teresa. We pray that by Thy merits and those of Thy beloved spouse, that we may receive a holy death burning with love for You.

Our Father...Hail Mary...Glory be...

St. Teresa, pray for us.

That we may become worthy of the promises of Christ.

Let us pray:

Graciously hear us, O God of our salvation, that as we rejoice in the commemoration of the blessed virgin Teresa, so we may be nourished by her heavenly doctrine, and obtain the fervour of tender devotion; through our Lord Jesus Christ, Thy Son, Who lives and reigns with Thee in the unity of the Holy Spirit, one God forever and ever. Amen.

ഇൗ✧ൽ

The ecstasy of St. Teresa

Quotations by St. Teresa

"It is foolish to think that we will enter Heaven
without entering into ourselves."

✧

"Untilled soil, however fertile it may be,
will bear thistles and thorns;
and so it is with man's mind."

✧

"Be gentle to all and stern with yourself."

✧

"Our body has this defect that,
the more it is provided care and comforts,
the more needs and desires it finds."

✧

"God aids the valiant...both to you and to me
He will give the help needed."

✧

"We can only learn to know ourselves
and do what we can, namely, surrender our will
and fulfil God's will in us."

✧

"I had many friends to help me to fall;
but as to rising again,
I was so much left to myself,
that I wonder now I was not
always on the ground.
I praise God for His mercy; for it was He only
Who stretched out His hand to me.
May He be blessed for ever! Amen."

✧

"What a great favour God does to those He places
in the company of good people!"

✧

"Accustom yourself continually
to make many acts of love,
for they enkindle and melt the soul."

✧

"Take God for your spouse and friend and walk
with Him continually, and you will not sin,
will learn to love, and the things you must do
will work out prosperously for you."

"We need no wings to go in search of Him, but have only to look upon Him present within us."

✧

"Contemplative prayer in my opinion is nothing else than a close sharing between friends; it means taking time frequently to be alone with Him Whom we know loves us."

✧

The tree that is beside the running water is fresher and gives more fruit.

✧

"The closer one approaches God, the simpler one becomes.

✧

To have courage for whatever comes in life – everything lies in that.

✧

You pay God a compliment by asking great things of Him.

৪০✧ଓ৪০✧ଓ৪০✧ଓ

Psalm 118. Beati immaculati.

(St. Peter d'Alcántara says for him this psalm is the perfect example that the end of all spiritual exercises and of all the spiritual life is obedience to the commandments of God and the accomplishment of the Divine Will. Therefore this psalm has been included in the Appendix. [+])

[+]   The Douay-Rheims translation is provided. The various headings, 'Aleph', 'Beth', etc., are the letters of the Hebrew alphabet. According to the Haydock commentary, St. Jerome expounded upon the significace of the letters, rendering them into a rough sentence in this order: 1. the doctrine. 2. of the house; 3. the plenitude, 4. of the tables (or holy scripture), 5. This 6. and 7. this 8. of life 9. a good 10. beginning, 11. the hand 12. of discipline (or the heart), 13. from them 14. everlasting 15. help, 16. the fountain (or eye) 17. of the mouth 18. of justice, 19. the calling 20. of the

Of the excellence of virtue consisting in the love and observance of the commandments of God. Alleluia.

ALEPH

(1) Blessed are the undefiled in the way, who walk in the law of the Lord. (2) Blessed are they that search his testimonies:[19] that seek him with their whole heart. (3) For they that work iniquity, have not walked in his ways. (4) Thou hast commanded thy commandments to be kept most diligently. (5) O! that my ways may be directed to keep thy justifications. (6) Then shall I not be confounded, when I shall look into all thy commandments. (7) I will praise thee with uprightness of heart, when I shall have learned the judgements of thy justice. (8) I will keep thy justifications: O! do not thou utterly forsake me.

---

head 21. of teeth 22. the signs.   Apparently, St. Jerome attempted to show by this symbolic rendering of the letters that the holy Scriptures bring us to the knowledge of the Church and of Christ   For further explanations of the verses of the psalm, the Haydock commentary is recommended.

19   "His testimonies": The commandments of God are called his testimonies, because they testify his holy will unto us. Note here, that in almost every verse of this psalm (which in number are 176) the word and law of God, and the love and observance of it, is perpetually inculcated, under a variety of denominations, all signifying the same thing. (Douay-Rheims).

BETH

(9) By what doth a young man correct his way? By observing thy words. (10) With my whole heart have I sought after thee: let me not stray from thy commandments. (11). Thy words have I hidden in my heart, that I may not sin against thee. (12) Blessed art thou, O Lord: teach me thy justifications. (13) With my lips I have pronounced all the judgements of thy mouth. (14) I have been delighted in the way of thy testimonies, as in all riches. (15). I will meditate on thy commandments: and I will consider thy ways. (16) I will think of thy justifications: I will not forget thy words.

GIMEL

(17) Give bountifully to thy servant, enliven me: and I shall keep thy words. (18) Open thou my eyes: and I will consider the wondrous things of thy law. (19) I am a sojourner on the earth: hide not thy commandments from me. (20). My soul hath coveted to long for thy justifications, at all times. (21) Thou hast rebuked the proud: they are cursed who decline from thy commandments. (22) Remove from me reproach and contempt: because I have sought after thy testimonies. (23) For princes sat, and spoke against me: but thy

servant was employed in thy justifications. (24) For thy testimonies are my meditation: and thy justifications my counsel.

DALETH

(25) My soul hath cleaved to the pavement: quicken thou me according to thy word. (26) I have declared my ways, and thou hast heard me: teach me thy justifications. (27) Make me to understand the way of thy justifications: and I shall be exercised in thy wondrous works. (28) My soul hath slumbered through heaviness: strengthen thou me in thy words. (29) Remove from me the way of iniquity: and out of thy law have mercy on me. (30) I have chosen the way of truth: thy judgements I have not forgotten. (31) I have stuck to thy testimonies, O Lord: put me not to shame. (32) I have run the way of thy commandments, when thou didst enlarge my heart.

HE

(33) Set before me for a law the way of thy justifications, O Lord: and I will always seek after it. (34). Give me understanding, and I will search thy law; and I will keep it with my whole heart. (35) Lead me into the path of thy commandments;

for this same I have desired. (36) Incline my heart into thy testimonies and not to covetousness. (37). Turn away my eyes that they may not behold vanity: quicken me in thy way. (38). Establish thy word to thy servant, in thy fear. (39) Turn away my reproach, which I have apprehended: for thy judgements are delightful. (40) Behold I have longed after thy precepts: quicken me in thy justice.

VAU

(41) Let thy mercy also come upon me, O Lord: thy salvation according to thy word. (42) So shall I answer them that reproach me in any thing; that I have trusted in thy words. (43) And take not thou the word of truth utterly out of my mouth: for in thy words, I have hoped exceedingly. (44) So shall I always keep thy law, for ever and ever. (45) And I walked at large: because I have sought after thy commandments. (46) And I spoke of thy testimonies before kings: and I was not ashamed. (47). I meditated also on thy commandments, which I loved. (48) And I lifted up my hands to thy commandments, which I loved: and I was exercised in thy justifications.

ZAIN

(49) Be thou mindful of thy word to thy servant, in which thou hast given me hope. (50) This hath comforted me in my humiliation: because thy word hath enlivened me. (51) The proud did iniquitously altogether: but I declined not from thy law. (52) I remembered, O Lord, thy judgements of old: and I was comforted. (53) A fainting hath taken hold of me, because of the wicked that forsake thy law. (54) Thy justifications were the subject of my song, in the place of my pilgrimage. (55) In the night I have remembered thy name, O Lord: and have kept thy law. (56) This happened to me: because I sought after thy justifications.

HETH

(57) O Lord, my portion, I have said, I would keep thy law. (58). I entreated thy face with all my heart: have mercy on me according to thy word. (59) I have thought on my ways: and turned my feet unto thy testimonies. (60) I am ready, and am not troubled: that I may keep thy commandments. (61) The cords of the wicked have encompassed me: but I have not forgotten thy law. (62) I rose at midnight to give praise to

thee; for the judgements of thy justification. (63) I am a partaker with all them that fear thee, and that keep thy commandments. (64) The earth, O Lord, is full of thy mercy: teach me thy justifications.

(65) Thou hast done well with thy servant, O Lord, according to thy word. (66) Teach me goodness and discipline and knowledge; for I have believed thy commandments. (67) Before I was humbled I offended; therefore have I kept thy word. (68) Thou art good; and in thy goodness teach me thy justifications. (69) The iniquity of the proud hath been multiplied over me: but I will seek thy commandments with my whole heart. (70) Their heart is curdled like milk: but I have meditated on thy law. (71) It is good for me that thou hast humbled me, that I may learn thy justifications. (72) The law of thy mouth is good to me, above thousands of gold and silver.

(73) Thy hands have made me and formed me: give me understanding, and I will learn thy commandments. (74) They that fear thee shall see me, and shall be glad: because I have greatly

hoped in thy words. (75). I know, O Lord, that thy judgements are equity: and in thy truth thou hast humbled me. (76) O! let thy mercy be for my comfort, according to thy word unto thy servant. (77) Let thy tender mercies come unto me, and I shall live: for thy law is my meditation. (78) Let the proud be ashamed, because they have done unjustly towards me: but I will be employed in thy commandments. (79). Let them that fear thee turn to me: and they that know thy testimonies. (80). Let my heart be undefiled in thy justifications, that I may not be confounded.

CAPH

(81) My soul hath fainted after thy salvation: and in thy word I have very much hoped. (82) My eyes have failed for thy word, saying: When wilt thou comfort me? (83) For I am become like a bottle in the frost: I have not forgotten thy justifications. (84). How many are the days of thy servant: when wilt thou execute judgement on them that persecute me? (85). The wicked have told me fables: but not as thy law. (86). All thy statutes are truth: they have persecuted me unjustly, do thou help me. (87) They had almost made an end of me upon earth: but I have not forsaken thy commandments. (88) Quicken thou me according to thy mercy: and I shall keep the testimonies of thy mouth.

LAMED

(89) For ever, O Lord, thy word standeth firm in heaven. (90) Thy truth unto all generations: thou hast founded the earth, and it continueth. (91). By thy ordinance the day goeth on: for all things serve thee. (92). Unless thy law had been my meditation, I had then perhaps perished in my abjection. (93). Thy justifications I will never forget: for by them thou hast given me life. (94) I am thine, save thou me: for I have sought thy justifications. (95) The wicked have waited for me to destroy me: but I have understood thy testimonies. (96) I have seen an end of all perfection: thy commandment is exceeding broad.

MEM

(97) O how have I loved thy law, O Lord! it is my meditation all the day. (98) Through thy commandment, thou hast made me wiser than my enemies: for it is ever with me. (99) I have understood more than all my teachers: because thy testimonies are my meditation. (100) I have had understanding above ancients: because I have sought thy commandments. (101) I have restrained my feet from every evil way: that I may keep thy words. (102) I have not declined from

thy judgements, because thou hast set me a law. (103) How sweet are thy words to my palate! more than honey to my mouth. (104) By thy commandments I have had understanding: therefore have I hated every way of iniquity.

NUN

(105) Thy word is a lamp to my feet, and a light to my paths. (106) I have sworn and am determined to keep the judgements of thy justice. (107) I have been humbled, O Lord, exceedingly: quicken thou me according to thy word. (108) The free offerings of my mouth make acceptable, O Lord: and teach me thy judgements. (109) My soul is continually in my hands: and I have not forgotten thy law. (110) Sinners have laid a snare for me: but I have not erred from thy precepts. (111) I have purchased thy testimonies for an inheritance for ever: because they are the joy of my heart. (112) I have inclined my heart to do thy justifications for ever, for the reward.

SAMECH

(113) I have hated the unjust: and have loved thy law. (114) Thou art my helper and my protector: and in thy word I have greatly hoped. (115) Depart from me, ye malignant: and I will

search the commandments of my God. (116) Uphold me according to thy word, and I shall live: and let me not be confounded in my expectation. (117) Help me, and I shall be saved: and I will meditate always on thy justifications. (118) Thou hast despised all them that fall off from thy judgements; for their thought is unjust. (119) I have accounted all the sinners of the earth prevaricators: therefore have I loved thy testimonies. (120) Pierce thou my flesh with thy fear: for I am afraid of thy judgements.

AIN

(121) I have done judgement and justice: give me not up to them that slander me. (122) Uphold thy servant unto good: let not the proud calumniate me. (123) My eyes have fainted after thy salvation: and for the word of thy justice. (124) Deal with thy servant according to thy mercy: and teach me thy justifications. (125) I am thy servant: give me understanding that I may know thy testimonies. (126) It is time, O Lord, to do: they have dissipated thy law. (127) Therefore have I loved thy commandments above gold and the topaz. (128) Therefore was I directed to all thy commandments: I have hated all wicked ways.

(129) Thy testimonies are wonderful: therefore my soul hath sought them. (130) The declaration of thy words giveth light: and giveth understanding to little ones. (131) I opened my mouth, and panted: because I longed for thy commandments. (132) Look thou upon me, and have mercy on me according to the judgement of them that love thy name. (133) Direct my steps according to thy word: and let no iniquity have dominion over me. (134) Redeem me from the calumnies of men: that I may keep thy commandments. (135) Make thy face to shine upon thy servant: and teach me thy justifications. (136) My eyes have sent forth springs of water: because they have not kept thy law.

SADE

(137) Thou art just, O Lord: and thy judgement is right. (138) Thou hast commanded justice thy testimonies: and thy truth exceedingly. (139) My zeal hath made me pine away: because my enemies forgot thy words. (140) Thy word is exceedingly refined: and thy servant hath loved it. (141) I am very young and despised; but I forget not thy justifications. (142) Thy justice is justice for ever: and thy law is the truth. (143) Trouble and anguish have found me: thy commandments

are my meditation. (144) Thy testimonies are justice for ever: give me understanding, and I shall live.

COPH

(145) I cried with my whole heart, hear me, O Lord: I will seek thy justifications. (146) I cried unto thee, save me: that I may keep thy commandments. (147) I prevented the dawning of the day, and cried: because in thy words I very much hoped. (148) My eyes to thee have prevented the morning: that I might meditate on thy words. (149) Hear thou my voice, O Lord, according to thy mercy: and quicken me according to thy judgement. (150) They that persecute me have drawn nigh to iniquity; but they are gone far off from thy law. (151) Thou art near, O Lord: and all thy ways are truth. (152) I have known from the beginning concerning thy testimonies: that thou hast founded them for ever.

RES

(153) See my humiliation and deliver me for I have not forgotten thy law. (154) Judge my judgement and redeem me: quicken thou me for thy word's sake. (155). Salvation is far from

sinners; because they have not sought thy justifications. (156) Many, O Lord, are thy mercies: quicken me according to thy judgement. (157) Many are they that persecute me and afflict me; but I have not declined from thy testimonies. (158) I beheld the transgressors, and pined away; because they kept not thy word. (159) Behold I have loved thy commandments, O Lord; quicken me thou in thy mercy. (160) The beginning of thy words is truth: all the judgements of thy justice are for ever.

SIN

(161) Princes have persecuted me without cause: and my heart hath been in awe of thy words. (162) I will rejoice at thy words, as one that hath found great spoil. (163) I have hated and abhorred iniquity; but I have loved thy law. (164) Seven times a day I have given praise to thee, for the judgements of thy justice. (165) Much peace have they that love thy law, and to them there is no stumbling block. (166) I looked for thy salvation, O Lord: and I loved thy commandments. (167) My soul hath kept thy testimonies and hath loved them exceedingly. (168). I have kept thy commandments and thy testimonies: because all my ways are in thy sight.

TAU

(169) Let my supplication, O Lord, come near in thy sight: give me understanding according to thy word. (170) Let my request come in before thee; deliver thou me according to thy word. (171) My lips shall utter a hymn, when thou shalt teach me thy justifications. (172) My tongue shall pronounce thy word: because all thy commandments are justice. (173) Let thy hand be with me to save me; for I have chosen thy precepts. (174) I have longed for thy salvation, O Lord; and thy law is my meditation. (175) My soul shall live and shall praise thee: and thy judgements shall help me. (176) I have gone astray like a sheep that is lost: seek thy servant, because I have not forgotten thy commandments.

෨✧ଓ

Illustration Credits

Page 28: *"Saint Teresa of Ávila Contemplating the Cross (1740-1750)"*, Domenico Maggiotto. Artvee - Public Domain listing.

Page 36: *"Esquisse pour l'église Saint-Louis-en-l'Ile : Jésus apparait à sainte Thérèse"* (1866) - (Child Jesus Appearing to St. Teresa), Lecomte-Vernet, Charles Emile Hippolyte (dit Émile Vernet-Lecomte). Paris Musées Collections.

Page 39: *"St Teresa of Avila Interceding for the Souls in Purgatory"*. Workshop of Peter Paul Rubens (Flemish, Siegen 1577–1640 Antwerp). Metropolitan Museum.

Page 42: *"St Teresa of Avila's Vision of the Dove"* (ca. 1650), Pierre van Schuppen. Metropolitan Museum.

Page 46: *"La comunión de Santa Teresa"* (Ca. 1670), Juan Martín Cabezalero (Spanish, 1633-1673). Artvee – Public Domain Listing.

Page 51: *"SS. Teresa and John of the Cross, with God the Father above"* (ca. 1690.) Anonymous, Spanish School, 17th century. Variant Attribution: manner of Antonio Palomino de Castro y Velasco, (1655-1726). Frick Digital Collections.

Page 54: *"St. Teresa Receiving a Necklace from the Virgin"* (after 1639), Gaspar de Crayer, (1584-1669). Frick Digital Collections.

Page 59: "*Primer Milagro De Santa Teresa De Jesús. Resurrección De Su Sobrino Don Gonzalo Ovalle, Hijo De Su Hermana Doña Juana De Ahumada,*" (1855). (First Miracle of St. Teresa of Jesus). Artvee – Public Domain.

Page 65: "*The Virgin Placing St. Teresa of Avila Under the Protection of St. Joseph*", (ca. 1787), François Guillaume Ménageot. Metropolitan Museum.

Page 67: "*St. Teresa de Jesús*" (1576), Juan de la Miseria. Frick Digital Collections.

Page 69: "*Extase van Teresa*", etching of the famous statue by Bernini. Print maker, Benoît Thiboust. Rijks Museum.

Page 75: "*Saint James The Greater With Saint Teresa Of Avila, The Coat Of Arms Of Castile And León Between Them*", (17th Century), School Of Madrid. Artvee – Public Domain.

Page 78: "*St. Theresa in Glory*", Bernardo Strozzi, (1581-1644). Frick Digital Collections.

Page 83: "*St. Teresa of Jesus Rewarded by Christ and the Virgin*", Pedro Orrente (1580-1645). Frick Digital Collections.

Page 86: "*Saint Teresa of Avila, (1644)*", Jusepe de Ribera (Spanish, 1591-1652). Artvee – Public Domain

Page 98: "*The Ecstasy of St. Teresa*" (ca. 1622–24), Antonius Wierix, II – Netherlandish. Metropolitan Museum.

Page 102: "Portret van Teresa van Avila" (1611 – 1613), Pieter de Jode (I), Rijks Museum.

**If you liked this book,
you will also like these
by Fr. Marin de Boylesve:**

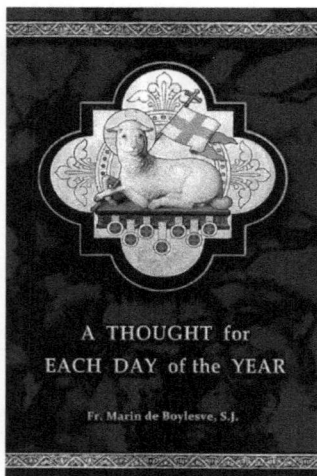

**A Thought for
Each Day of the Year**

ISBN: 978-989-33-1995-6

**The Blessed Virgin
According to the Gospels**

ISBN: 978-989-5372607

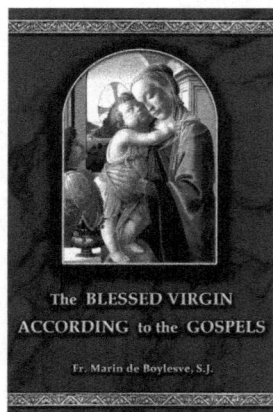

The Sacred Heart
of Jesus

ISBN: 978-989-33-2807-1

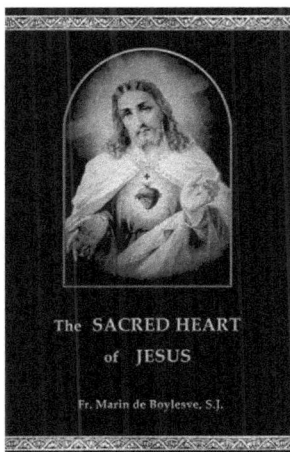

The Month
of the Precious Blood

ISBN: 978-989-33-2808-8

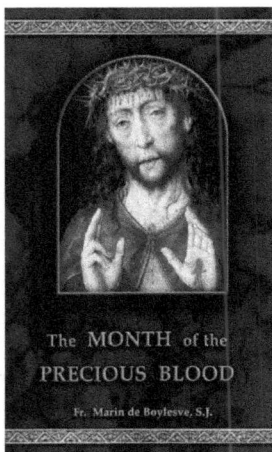

**Little Month
of Saint Joseph**

ISBN: 978-989-96844-8-5

**The Month
of Saint Michael**

ISBN: 978-989-96844-9-2